Reading With GOD In Mind

J.K. Jones

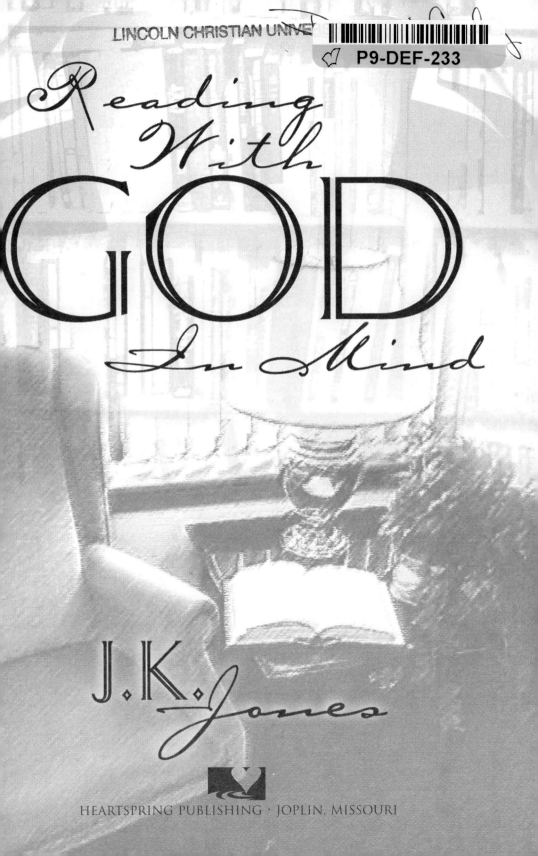

HEARTSPRING PUBLISHING · JOPLIN, MISSOURI

Cover Design by Mark A. Cole

Library of Congress Cataloging-in-Publication Data

Jones, J. K. (John Kenneth), 1953–
    Reading with God in mind / by J. K. Jones, Jr.
        p.   cm.
Includes bibliographical references.
    ISBN 0-89900-936-0 (pbk.)
    1. Christian life.   2. Books and reading—Religious aspects—Christianity.   I. Title.
    BV4501.3.J647 2003
    248.4—dc22

                                                          2003014849

Dedcation and Gratitude

Mom — I thank God in heaven for you. You never gave up on me.
You cheered me on when I thought I would never read.
You have blessed me.

Mom Graham — I praise God for your faithfulness and selflessness.
You have found many books that have fed my soul.
You have refreshed me.

Mom Harper — I worship God who brought you into my life.
You have encouraged me to keep growing.
You have inspired me.

Special thanks to Dr. Tom Tanner, academic dean of Lincoln Christian College and Seminary, for proofing this book and simply being my friend. I "acknowledge this with profound gratitude" (Acts 24:3). Finally, to Sue, Lindsey, and Chelsea, I am forever grateful for your support and love. I love you "bigger than the sky."

Table of Contents

Introduction

This is a book about readers and for those who wish to become readers.
Particularly, it is for readers of books.
Even more particularly, it is for those whose main purpose
in reading books is to gain increased understanding
(Mortimer J. Adler and Charles Van Doren, *How to Read a Book*, p. 3).

So why do some of us love to read? One possible answer might be, "We read in order to know that we are not alone." I have been meditating on that eloquent sentence since I first heard it uttered in the movie, *Shadowlands.*

Perhaps you saw that motion picture. It documents the story of C.S. Lewis. In a pivotal scene, Lewis leads a discussion with his students on their assigned reading. He asks the question, "Why do we read?" One of the young men, who seems less than motivated, quotes what his father once said to him, "We read in order to know that we are not alone." It causes Lewis, played by Anthony Hopkins, to stop and carefully consider the weight of the statement.

There are a number of reasons why I read. For example, as a teacher and preacher I want to stay abreast of my field of study, and I want to grow in my knowledge and understanding of Scripture. I also simply enjoy the escape that reading affords me. I get to hear from people I would never have the opportunity to meet face to face. Through my reading I also enjoy the privilege of traveling to places where I might never be permitted to go. There is, however, a more fundamental reason. Life can be cruel and it can be lonely. When I pick up a book, touch its cover, turn its pages, listen to its words, meditate on its ideas, I begin to realize that I am not alone. There is another human being out there who speaks my language, understands my heart, and expresses the thoughts that I sometimes have when mine seem so jumbled and garbled. Now and then, a wonderfully intimate moment occurs that is worth the effort. Ultimately, behind the words on the printed page of a book I hear God speaking to me.

I periodically grow frustrated with my lack of spiritual maturity. I want to move beyond my infantlike state and grow into the person of God that my Creator longs for me to be. I begin to look for quick solutions. I go to a conference because I have heard that a particular speaker is inspiring and offers to reveal a secret to Christian growth. But when I pick up a book like *Power through Prayer* by E.M. Bounds and I read these words, I believe that God too is speaking to me about my easy Christianity: "God's acquaintance is not made by pop calls. God does not bestow His gifts on the casual or hasty comers and goers. Much time with God alone is the secret of knowing Him and of influence with Him. He yields to the persistency of a faith that knows Him" (Bounds, pp. 33-34). It is as if Bounds is having a private conversation with me!

Oswald Chambers: "The author who benefits you most is not the one who tells you something you did not know before, but the one who gives expression to the truth that has been dumbly struggling in you for utterance."
My Utmost for His Highest, Dec. 16 reading

Blaise Pascal: "I can only approve of those who seek God with groans."
A Mind on Fire, p. 118

This book is intended to target two specific groups of people. First, I want to coach those who have begun a life of reading and simply need some encouragement to continue the journey. I especially want to cheer them on and offer a word or two of

INTRODUCTION

humble advice. Second, I want to challenge those who, like some of my students, are not convinced that reading books is all that important and beneficial. I know how ironic that sounds. I'm assuming, though, that some will read this book because a teacher or friend has asked them, not because they really want to read. They find reading boring and prefer a medium other than the printed page. For those of you in this group I have designed a book that is brief, informative, and hopefully engaging. This book is a "why, how, and so what?" book. I want to help you find your own reading glasses or clean the ones that may have gotten dirty over time. Come along with me. Possibly your experience will be like that of Thomas à Kempis. "I sought for rest but never found it, save in a little corner with a little book" (*The Imitation of Christ*, p. 5).

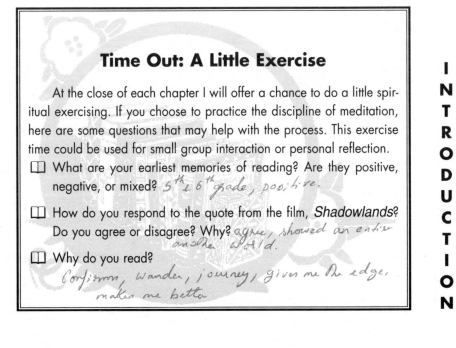

Time Out: A Little Exercise

At the close of each chapter I will offer a chance to do a little spiritual exercising. If you choose to practice the discipline of meditation, here are some questions that may help with the process. This exercise time could be used for small group interaction or personal reflection.

☐ What are your earliest memories of reading? Are they positive, negative, or mixed? 5th & 6th grade, positive.

☐ How do you respond to the quote from the film, *Shadowlands*? Do you agree or disagree? Why? agree, showed an entire another world.

☐ Why do you read?
Confirms, wander, journey, gives me the edge, makes me better

1

Take up and Read: First Things First

Reading books comes naturally for Christians. Of course, the primer for all reading is the Word of God. Together, we confess, "We are people of one Book." Yet, our reading is not limited to the Bible. We read book after book, which helps us understand and apply the Word of God.
In the last half of the twentieth century particularly, the publishing of Christian books became a major industry, offering readers thousands of titles at reasonable cost.
Although we are reading more, we may not be reading what is best (David L. McKenna, *How to Read a Christian Book*, pp. 11-12).

I love to read. My unashamed declaration of dependence is that I could not live in a world where reading was not allowed. In Ray Bradbury's world of *Fahrenheit 451* (the temperature at which paper burns), firemen are paid to start fires rather than stop them. It's a time when books are for burning, not for reading. Then that fateful day arrives when Montag, a fireman with ten years experience, arrives at a home where books have been hidden away and must be destroyed. The firemen break into the attic where the books tumble down on top of them. A page of one of the books hangs open long enough for Montag to read a line, "but it blazed in his mind for the next minute as if stamped there with fiery steel" (p. 37). I can break out into a cold sweat just thinking of a society without good books to read. Much of who I am is wrapped up in the binding of books I've read, reread, and read again. I am an unembarrassed addict. You wouldn't know it by looking at me. There are no needle marks on my arms, no nervous twitch on my face, and no telltale scent that would give away my secret. Since the day the words on my first grade reader came alive to me I have reveled in reading. Who could have guessed that *"See Dick. See Jane. See Sally."* could have been so life changing?

I confess that there was a time when I would sneak off to the public library in order to digest one more slice from the delicious dessert tray of Mark Twain or Robert Louis Stevenson. I didn't want anyone to know about my library sweet tooth. It wasn't fashionable or socially acceptable to be known as a "bookworm" on the grade-school playground. A kid could get beat up for that kind of thing. Children in my hometown ostracized and excluded readers. It certainly wasn't smart to tell my football and baseball buddies that I delighted in reading as much as kicking and throwing a ball. I am now old enough to acknowledge that a day well-spent for me includes the companionship of a trusted book. I thoroughly enjoy sipping a raspberry mocha latte, at one of the local Barnes and Noble bookstores, while sitting in a comfortable chair and downing a recently published novel or an old classic. Words, sentences, paragraphs, and chapters whisk me away to a world that I've never visited before. I delight in climbing aboard the magic carpet ride of a well-written book.

Oswald Chambers: "My books! I cannot tell you what they are to me— silent, wealthy, loyal lovers. To look at them, to handle them, and to re-read them! I do thank God for my books with every fibre of my being. Friends that are ever true and ever your own." *Abandoned to God*, pp. 108-109

Not Just Any Kind of Book

I wouldn't be far off if I generalized about this one notion: reading has fallen on hard times. I'm not talking about the kind of reading that captures popular culture. Reading for escape or for personal advancement is soaring. Even

CHAPTER ONE

secondhand bookstores are on the rise (see "Snapshots" in *USA Today*, September 18, 2002, p. 10). The news media has put it well. "A short history of literacy could go like this: Gutenberg, King James, libraries, and Oprah. . . . Along came talk-show titan Oprah and her book club, inspiring the masses to read a wider range of books including several by previously little-known authors" ("Oprah Chapter Ends" in *USA Today*, April 12, 2002, p. 13A). The book club kind of reading has a legitimate place in the whole discussion, but I am talking about the kind of reading that turns the heart to consider, contemplate, and change. I am talking about the kind of reading that challenges the mind to think Christianly. I am referring to the kind of reading that nourishes the soul toward Christian maturity. I am describing the kind of reading that inspires the reader toward Christian service. Lest I be misunderstood, I am primarily preoccupied with the lack of Bible reading these days, though this book will address other kinds of reading as well. Please don't think of this concern as just another complaint. I'm chuckling to myself right now, even as I write. Sometimes I laugh for fear that I will soon be overcome with tears. I wonder if anyone will even read this puny book, let alone God's Magna Carta?

God's Book has become a dead book for many Christians. If you have read your Bible through from Genesis to Revelation, you are in the minority. If you have systematically read through it, you are a member of a very exclusive society. Each semester I take an unscientific poll of my students. I ask how many of them have read the Bible from cover to cover. Every year the percentage shrinks to a smaller and smaller number. This is heartbreaking to me. I wonder what God thinks of it? I do believe that God longs to be known. He

God longs to be known through His Word.

**C
H
A
P
T
E
R

O
N
E**

has, out of His abundant heart, given us a means to know Him. By the power and presence of the Holy Spirit, He has moved men in various times and places in order to get His message heard (Heb 1:1-2; 2 Pet 1:19-21). He even went so far as to flesh out that message in Jesus Christ (John 1:14). What a gift! George Mueller knew the life-changing power of reading the Book. Somewhere in my devotional time I came across these challenging and stretching lines of his: "It has been my habit to read the Bible through four times a year, in a prayerful spirit, to apply it to my heart, and practice what I find there. I have been a happy man; happy, happy, happy."

My Heritage and the Book

My Christian heritage has placed great emphasis upon the Bible as our sufficient rule of faith and practice. We have underscored the importance of coming within listening distance of God. I confess that I did not read the Bible through and absorb its implications for my life until I was twenty years old. I was raised and nurtured in a Christian home and in the local church, but somewhere I never quite grasped the eternal significance of reading the Scriptures. I read Greek mythology, praised Shakespeare, respected Thoreau, and honored the great books and authors of the Western World. I nearly missed my Creator in the beauty of His creation.

If you are a reader of Church History, you may know the story of Augustine's conversion. In AD 386 he found himself sitting on a park bench in Milan. He heard a voice say, "Take up and read. Take up and read." He opened the Bible and read Romans 13:11-14, concluding that God was calling him to give up his life of rebellion and come to faith in Christ. God, I believe, is once again calling people to "Take up and

read." John Wesley, of eighteenth-century fame, found himself frustrated over the lack of reading among Christian leaders. He told young ministers of his day to read or get out of the ministry. He clearly understood what was at stake.

When I initiate conversations about reading, someone inevitably asks the question: "How many books have you read?" I usually respond, "I don't have the foggiest notion how many books I've read." That information is totally unimportant. What is really vital and essential is the digestion and application of the one eternal Book. Christians are to be a people of one Book. Perhaps a word of caution and reminder would be appropriate before concluding. "Even though Christians are people of one Book, we are not guilty of what some critics call 'Bibliolatry.' We read the written Word, but we do not worship it" (David McKenna, *How to Read a Christian Book*, p. 21). The best book is the one that leads the soul out into the daylight and points that soul toward the Celestial City. The Bible is that book! My prayer is that it would be your book.

The best book is the one that leads the soul out into the daylight and points that soul toward the Celestial City.

Some Simple Guidelines

Here are some simple guidelines that may help you to foster a lifelong holy habit of daily Bible reading.

1. Find a quiet place to go to where you can regularly read. Elaine McEwan says, "Both adults and children need special places to keep their books and to curl up and read" (*How to Raise a Reader*, p. 140). If this encouragement is important for reading books in general, why wouldn't it be even more so of God's Book?
2. If you are new at Bible reading, start small. Read ten to

fifteen minutes each day. Aim for reading a section of Scripture or a solitary chapter. Don't hurry. Work at cultivating the ability to listen deeply. The ancients called this practice, *lectio divina*. It is a slow, contemplative practice of praying and pondering the Scriptures you are reading. Select one of the Gospels as a place to start. Listen with the ears of your heart. If you have been practicing this spiritual exercise for some time, stretch yourself. Read through the Bible a couple of times a year. Read from a variety of translations for freshness. Change your pace of reading now and then in order to avoid staleness.

3. Savor what you are reading. If the book is yours, use a pen to underline and circle words and sentences that speak to your heart. It is a good practice to keep a journal about what you discover in your reading. Note the questions that surface while you read. Come back to those questions later for further reflection and prayer.

4. Talk with another Jesus-follower about what you read. I appreciate the wisdom of Eugene Peterson. "For Christians the Bible is the primary book for spiritual reading. In the course of reading Scripture, it is only natural that we fall into conversation with friends who are also reading it" (Peterson, *Take and Read*, p. x).

5. Ask God to give you an ever-increasing spiritual appetite for His Book. He honors this kind of prayer. There is ample testimony that our Father takes great delight in giving us a greater hunger and a larger thirst for Him (Ps 42:1-2).

6. Select a devotional book companion to supplement your Bible reading. Some of the best resources would include Oswald Chamber's *My Utmost for His Highest*, Charles

Spurgeon's *Morning and Evening*, Fred Buechner's *Listening to Your Life*, or Bob and Michael Benson's, *Disciplines for the Inner Life*.

Consider this. How can we worship a God that we don't know? Take up and read! How can we live a life worthy of the grace given us at the cross if we don't know what our Lord desires? Take up and read! How can we ever experience the first hand joy of hearing God speak directly to us of His purpose and plan? Take up and read! How will we ever know that He is a universal God? Take up and read! How will we ever grasp that God's people have universal responsibilities? Take up and read! How will we ever know that God is not white, red, yellow, black, or brown? Take up and read! Please, for the sake of the Kingdom, a watching world, and your soul, take up and read!

Time Out: A Little Exercise

☐ Why do you think that most Christians in the western world don't spend much time reading their Bibles? *instant gratification, media numbness*

☐ What part of the chapter spoke most deeply to you? *Guidlines "listen with ear" of you*

☐ Do you have a reading plan that regularly takes you through the pages of Scripture?

☐ What has the Lord recently impressed upon your heart from your Bible reading?

☐ If you don't have a systematic plan for reading the Word, here are some suggestions:

Pick up "McCheyne's Calendar for Daily Readings." Try reading through the *One Year Bible* or some other published guide easily found in your nearest Christian bookstore. An on-line plan can be found at **www.discipleshipjournal.com**.

C
H
A
P
T
E
R

O
N
E

2
Searching for Wisdom

There is some feeling nowadays that reading is not as necessary as it once was. . . . But it may be seriously questioned whether the advent of modern communications media has much enhanced our understanding of the world in which we live. . . . There is a sense in which we moderns are inundated with facts to the detriment of understanding
(Adler, *How to Read a Book*, pp. 3-4).

Alan Jacobs, a professor of English at Wheaton College in Illinois, has written a weighty and important work on reading entitled *A Theology of Reading*. Dr. Jacobs reflects on a crucial question. If the Christian life is to be shaped and molded by the "law of love," to love God and neighbor, what would it mean to read lovingly? It is such a marvelous question. I want to become a charitable reader developing my intellectual skill while practicing the law of love. I sometimes fail miserably in living this life of love.

For example, a while back I got angry in class. I am sorry about that and apologized to the students as well. I've done a great deal of team teaching these past few years with a very dear friend of mine. We've known each other twenty years. I love my Christian brother immensely. I suppose that explains why I became so upset. My colleague was attempting to lead the class in reflecting on the assigned reading for the day. He was inviting all of us to dialogue about things of such immense importance for ministry and mission. He was getting nowhere, knee-deep in academic mud. It soon became apparent that these precious students had not completed their reading! For me it was a character issue. I told them so! Of course, the room became very quiet. I felt especially sorry for my friend standing there in front of that rebuked bunch and looking as if he were praying for Jesus to immediately return. After my apology the students opened up a bit even if they had not read the material! I know that staying on top of one's required reading is quite demanding, and it got me wondering about how difficult it is to read simply for the cultivation of one's own soul. I'm not looking for more facts. I'm searching for wisdom.

A Speaking God

God speaks. Go back and read that sentence again. Do I have your attention? I know that I can get myself into trouble if I'm not careful with those first two words. It might be good, from the start, to tell you what I don't mean when I say that God speaks. I don't mean that God is adding new revelation to Scripture. I know that there are certain "religious" groups

God speaks. Does He have your attention?

that hold to the notion that God has added or is adding further to what He has already spoken in Scripture. I'm not one of those. I do mean, though, that at God's very core He is a revealing God. He wants to be known and can be known (Jer 9:23-24; Hos 6:6; John 17:25-26; Acts 17:24-28). What I also mean is that God has spoken to us in times past through the Prophets. He can still bring a fresh word to us from those ancient spokesmen as we study, meditate, and pray. The Bible testifies to the fact that God has spoken to us ultimately in our Savior, Jesus Christ (Heb 1:1-2). I have devoted my life, perhaps you have also, to listening, understanding, and applying what God has said about His Son. Reverence for Him is the first step towards wisdom (Prov 1:7).

C H A P T E R

T W O

I assume you already know by now that I love to read. What I haven't told you is that I believe God can speak to us clearly through other books we read if we allow the Scriptures to be the lens through which we determine and evaluate all of our reading. I do not waver one whit on the fact that the Bible is the foundation and center of all that I read. What I want to talk about with you is the profound and powerful place good books can have in helping us to listen for God. He does speak through our reading.

A Starting Place

Marcus Aurelius: "From Rusticus, I received the impression that my character required improvement and discipline; and from him I learned . . . to read carefully, and not to be satisfied with a superficial understanding of a book. . . ." *The Meditations of Marcus Aurelius, 1:7*

The kind of reading that I'm suggesting is the sort that nourishes the soul, inspires the mind, and moves the body to Christian service. I believe this to be the best kind of reading. So where does one begin? There are so many books out there. Over one thousand are printed each week! Many of those would not help your soul and might do serious damage to it. A.W. Tozer speaks of "harmful books."

By harmful books I do not mean those on a high intellectual level, such as the classics, poetry, history, political science and whatever falls within the category of the liberal arts. I mean cheap fiction (religious or secular), shallow religious chop suey such as is found in so many religious magazines and the world of religious trash designed to entertain the saints. Of course, I include under the designation of harmful books the vulgar and the unclean (*The Size of the Soul*, p. 34).

CHAPTER TWO

How exactly should we avoid selecting the "harmful books"? The best piece of reading advice I ever received came from my friend, Jackina Stark, who teaches at Ozark Christian College. She simply said, "Pray." Now that's wisdom! You and I need to humbly ask God to direct us to the best books. John Baillie prayed this way:

> Leave me not, O gracious Presence, in such hours as I may today devote to the reading of books or of newspapers. Guide my mind to choose the right books and, having chosen them, to read them in the right way. When I read for profit, grant that all I read may lead me nearer to Thyself. When I read for recreation, grant that what I read may not lead me away from Thee. Let all my reading so refresh my mind that I may the more eagerly seek after whatsoever things are pure and fair and true (*A Diary of Private Prayer*, p. 89).

Prayer is the best way to begin reading.

A second suggestion for reading would be to seek the wisdom of other readers. I do not mean for this to sound egotistical or harsh, but I have wondered why so many Christians today seem to enjoy and prefer such shallow reading. I don't say that with a mean or combative spirit. I know we all begin our reading journey at different places. Like a baby that has to move from her mother's milk to solid food, so readers must grow in their appetite for spiritual food that strengthens and matures. The most often read devotional books have little muscle and vitality in them. Maybe all of this has something to do with the lack of good advice. David McKenna, in *How to Read A Christian Book*, Susan Annette Muto, in *A Practical Guide to Spiritual Reading*, and Eugene Peterson, in *Take and Read*, all offer

superb coaching on what books to read. Sometimes just talking with other readers introduces us to books that are worthy of our consideration and time. The process does not need to be complicated. I have been directed to other books simply by noticing what books are being quoted in the volume I am currently reading or by paying attention to footnotes.

Readers must grow in their appetite for spiritual food that strengthens and matures.

You know by now that I teach at a Bible college. It is a fine school. I serve with some wonderful people. I believe that we have some exceptional students studying at Lincoln Christian College just as I believe that there are exceptional students elsewhere. Yet, more and more, I encounter young people who have never read any of the great devotional writers (Augustine, Law, Thomas à Kempis, Bernard of Clairvaux, Bunyan, Teresa of Avila, Madame Guyon, etc.), let alone reread and truly absorbed them. I consistently meet people in local congregations who no longer take the time to digest and grow from good books. These dear Christian people have created desertlike conditions within their own inner landscapes. Spiritual reading was once viewed as one of the primary gardening tools for the soul. Every matter that concerns God and my relationship with Him must begin on bended knees. If I do not thirst for the best books and am inclined to not read at all, then I need to implore God to forgive me and revive my dull mind and whet my thirst for spiritual matters. Tozer has helped me enormously in my pursuit of the best books. Here is another gem of great wisdom.

Remember that reading is hearing with the mind. . . . Observe Bacon's famous rule: "Read not to contradict and confute, nor to believe and take for granted, nor to find talk and discourse, but to

C
H
A
P
T
E
R

T
W
O

weigh and consider. Some books are to be tasted, others to be swallowed, and some few to be chewed and digested" (*The Size of The Soul*, pp. 44 & 50).

I must ask God to direct my attention to that kind of book. Maybe this is what the Apostle Paul had in mind when he wrote Timothy his second letter. The old preacher and evangelist is jailed in a Roman prison. He is cold, weary from all of his travels, and lonely. He tells Timothy, "When you come, bring the cloak that I left with Carpus at Troas, and my scrolls, especially the parchments" (2 Tim 4:13). Other than a coat to keep warm and a friend to talk to, he wants books (*biblia*) and the parchments (*membranes*). We don't know exactly what he meant by those two terms. Whatever he was asking for, whether his own writings, Old Testament Scriptures, or both, Paul needed his books. John Stott is correct, "When our spirit is lonely, we need friends. When our body is cold, we need clothing. When our mind is bored, we need books. To admit this is not unspiritual; it is human" (*Guard the Gospel*, p. 121). Amen.

CHAPTER TWO

A Simple Challenge

A number of years ago I was sitting in church minding my own business and trying to remain attentive to the sermon. I noticed that a young girl directly in front of me was reading Garrett Sheldon's, *What Would Jesus Do?* The book is a contemporary retelling of the old classic by Garrett's great-grandfather Charles, entitled *In His Steps*. I know that there is an appropriate time for everything, including reading. I was not bothered by her timing. I found myself greatly encouraged. Here was someone so small reading something

that was so large. I appreciated that, even if it was being read in church. You probably should know that the man sitting to my left was asleep! While my neighbor slept, I took pen in hand and wrote the child a note on my worship bulletin. This is what I told her.

> You may not know me. My name is J.K. Jones and I love to read. I noticed you were reading a very good book based on one of the first "classics" I ever read. Please keep reading good books like this one. God will speak to your heart and remind you of what He has already said in the best book, the Bible.

Please don't attack this little one or me. I'm not putting her book above preaching. She will understand as the days go by that God does speak when His Word is preached, and she will learn to be attentive (1 Sam 3:1-10). Let's give her a chance to get the right idea about God. In the meantime why not ask, "Am I listening for God?"

Time Out: A Little Exercise

📖 How does a person become a charitable reader?

📖 What method do you use in selecting the books that you will read?

📖 What part of this chapter spoke to your heart?

📖 Has God spoken to you through the reading of good books? If so, what has been your experience?

📖 How do you respond to my definition of the best kind of reading? It is the kind that "nourishes the soul, inspires the reader, and moves the reader to Christian service."

CHAPTER TWO

3

Turning Pages in Silence

We are in some danger of believing that the speed and wizardry of our gadgets have freed us from the sometimes arduous work of turning pages in silence (Sven Birkerts, *The Gutenberg Elegies: The Fate of Reading in an Electronic Age*, p. 32).

The soul and good books are a match made in heaven. They work together to form and shape a strong inner life. Daily doses of lust, pride, stress, and various forms of seduction can and will sabotage the soul. Like you, I find myself journeying through a world that elevates wealth, health, technology, and information. That same world diminishes contentment, solitude, service, and wisdom. When the God of the universe called this world into existence, He created everything from light to land. All of it was good according to the biblical account. The day the Lord fashioned man and woman was a very good day! I regularly read through those accounts in Genesis 1 & 2, John 1, and Colossians 1. I find myself refreshed and affirmed as I digest and ruminate on the scriptural promise that I have been wonderfully and mysteriously crafted. Yet, in all that artistic and imaginative design, God intentionally left out a few things. I'm sure you've noticed this. Our heavenly Father did not set aside a single day of creation for inventing stress, worry, or hurry. These are enemies to the life centered on Jesus.

24-Hour Restlessness

We are a 24-hour society. We overeat and undersleep. We shoot up and break down. We surf the Net and starve the soul. We seek out shallow intimacy and throw out responsibility. We worship at the altar of Wall Street and take the detour around Church Street. We buy cellular phones, personal computers, and handy beepers in order to save time. We tend to download and overload. We shop 'til we drop. We buy now and pay later. We watch the clock, but fail to watch the Christ. Every hour that goes by we find ourselves sucked deeper into the muck and mire of technology's seduction. Gandhi was right: There is more to life than increasing its speed.

But I have stilled and quieted my soul; / like a weaned child with its mother, / like a weaned child is my soul with me. Ps 131:2, NIV

The Christian life, according to Eugene Peterson, is a recovery of what was lost in the Fall. I want to recover what God intended for my soul. Yes, I know that in Christ I am a new creation (2 Cor 5:17). I believe that Jesus now lives in me (Col 2:20) and that the Holy Spirit comforts, guides, and instructs the child of God (John 14:15ff; 16:5ff; Rom 8:1ff). All of this is true and I praise God for it! But I am plagued by lost confidence, misplaced cooperation, minimal compassion, and depleted communion. Just like you I find myself in a daily life-and-death battle even though the war has already been won. What a strange condition: to be victorious in Christ and still have the capacity to lose my own soul. Good books can collect dust in times like these. The crisis of our time makes us feel utterly hopeless. To suggest that the reading of a good book might shift the momentum toward revival seems childish.

History and Devotional Reading

I am attempting to think with you about the place of reading in maturing us into Christlikeness. James Means has carefully observed that more information has come into existence in the last three decades than in the previous five thousand years. Every twelve months the average American reads 3,000 notices and forms, 100 newspapers, and 36 magazines. That same average American annually consumes 2,463 hours in watching television, 730 hours listening to the radio, and 61 hours talking on the telephone (Means, *Effective Pastors for a New Century*, pp. 51-52). In this kind of

T. S. Eliot: "Where is the wisdom we have lost in knowledge? Where is the knowledge we have lost in information?" *from "Choruses from the Rock"*

mess I am humbly declaring for anyone who will listen that a good book can help us slow down, sit down, and settle down. Remember to dine at the table of books that nourish the soul, inspire the mind, and move you toward Christian service. Good, wholesome, invigorating spiritual reading is being exchanged for

technical manuals. My soul and your soul need more wisdom, not more information. Again, listen to Tozer.

> A book is a reservoir in which the raw material of thought is stored, a channel through which ideas are piped from one mind to another. . . . Books and money are alike in that they are useless when hoarded. Each has a purpose and is valuable only when allowed to fulfill that purpose. . . . The people of God should run to these [great religious classics of the past] as a thirsting stag runs to bury his muzzle in the cooling stream (*The Size of the Soul*, pp. 36-37 and p. 48).

I am praying for a great awakening. Some of you are praying that same prayer. The recovery of devotional reading has aroused sleeping saints in the past. Augustine read Antony of Egypt. Luther read Tauler. Wesley read Fenelon

C H A P T E R   T H R E E

and Thomas à Kempis. Spurgeon read anything he could get his hands on. C.S. Lewis began to read George MacDonald, George Herbert, John Bunyan, and Jeremy Taylor. His life was forever altered. I don't recall the first time I picked up a book by Lewis, but I do remember the delight I found when I read his *Screwtape Letters*. Maybe you've read it. It is a fictional story filled with conversations between a senior devil and his young understudy. The junior tempter is being instructed and exhorted to entice a man to turn from God's way. The older demon pushes the younger one to do all that he can to keep the man in question from intimacy with Christ. "Get him away from the Enemy," commands the senior devil. After some time elapses the understudy returns and reports, "We lost him, he has gone all the way over to the Enemy's side." "How did that happen?" asks the chief tempter. "He started to take a long walk every morning, just for the pleasure of it, and the Enemy found him more receptive," replied the younger demon. In disgust and anger the crusty senior replies, "That's where you blew it. If you had only had him walk for the sake of exercise, it would have become dreaded and tedious, devoid of pleasure. If you had only had him reading so he could parrot the contents to someone else, reading would become burdensome and boring rather than pleasurable. We could then have easily snared him!"

> In our Maker's wide mercy and deep grace He gave us the Bible.

God delights in books! He took His own words and put them into print. When time comes to an end, all of the universe will conclude that He wrote the very best one! In our Maker's wide mercy and deep grace He gave us the Bible. His Book, through the Holy Spirit, can illuminate our path and light the way toward reading, critiquing, and benefiting from other books. The

CHAPTER THREE

reading of books was never intended to elevate self. There is no place for arrogance in the life of the reader. I want to remind you that the whole world is written down in books. Books are like eggs that must be cracked open in order to get at the nourishment inside. Our Father, the Cosmic Farmer of the soul, gave us a tool to cultivate our inner life and better serve His creation. Thank God for good books! Thank God for those who read and apply them! I thank God for those who read with a spirit of love. I thank God for anyone who does the arduous work of turning pages in silence.

Time Out: A Little Exercise

☐ What books and authors have cultivated your inner life?

☐ How have you come to understand the challenge we face in keeping our inner life healthy and vibrant? What is positive about technology's influence on the soul and what is negative? How can we manage the information overload?

☐ Do you think the kind of reading being encouraged in this book can help foster a spiritual awakening in this country? Why?

4

A Good Question Is Worth a Thousand Answers

The rules for reading yourself to sleep are easier to follow than are the rules for staying awake while reading. Get into bed in a comfortable position, make sure the light is inadequate enough to cause a slight eyestrain, choose a book that is either terribly difficult or terribly boring—in any event, one that you do not really care whether you read or not—and you will be asleep in a few minutes. . . . If your aim in reading is to profit from it—to grow somehow in mind or spirit—you have to keep awake. That means reading as actively as possible (Adler, *How to Read a Book*, p. 45).

When I was a freshman in Bible college, I took a course called "Written Communication." The class was designed not only to teach the student good writing skills, but also to enable the student to learn to ask the right questions when reading someone else's writing. The assigned textbook for the course was Mortimer J. Adler and Charles Van Doren's, *How to Read a Book*. The subtitle of the book is *The Classic Guide to Intelligent Reading*. Most of us in that semester's adventure were shocked by the weight and breadth of the book. I'm not simply talking about its four-hundred-plus pages. I'm talking about its subject matter. It took our very best ability and much encouragement from our instructor to get through that formidable volume. Yet, something richly positive happened to me in that course that I have never gotten over. I complained as much as the next person about reading Adler, but my life, particularly my reading, has been forever marked by that freshman course. It was in the reading of a book about how to read a book that I learned to become an active reader! Christopher Morley recognizes what is at stake. He says, "The real purpose of books is to trap the mind into doing its own thinking" (*Handbook of Contemporary Preaching*, edited by Michael Duduit, p. 487). Walt Whitman understood the necessity for being an alert reader. "Books are to be called for, and supplied, on the assumption that the process of reading is not a half sleep, but, in the highest sense, an exercise, a gymnast's struggle; that the reader is to do something for himself, must be on the alert. . . . Not that the book needs so much to be the complete thing, but the reader of the book does" (*The Portable Whitman*, ed. Mark Van Doren, p. 468). It was Adler who helped me to understand that a good question is worth a thousand answers. Every reader needs to learn to ask four fundamental questions while they read.

Questions to Ask

First, *do I understand what I am reading*? This is the fundamental question that every reader must answer. Adler calls this the elementary level of reading (p. 17). There is an example of this kind of reading in the New Testament, specifically in Acts 8. A man we know as the Ethiopian eunuch had been worshiping in Jerusalem and was returning home. Dr. Luke tells us that this man was an important official in charge of all the treasury of Candace, queen of the Ethiopians (8:27). The eunuch was reading from the book of Isaiah, somewhere in chapter 53. Apparently he didn't understand what he was reading because Philip the Evangelist had been instructed by the Holy Spirit to approach the chariot where the man was sitting. Philip asked him the question that every reader must ask: "Do you understand what you are reading?" The eunuch responded, "How can I unless someone explains it to me?"

Do I understand what I am reading?

C H A P T E R

F O U R

BOOKS

I regularly ask this question of the book I am reading. Sometimes I'll write the question in the front of the book and jot down my response. It helps me to read with an active mind. Some books are difficult to understand because of the topic, the author's writing style, or the reader's lack of familiarity with the material. One of the most difficult books I have ever read is a devotional classic called *The Cloud of Unknowing*, a fourteenth-century English work. We don't know who wrote it. It seems to be all about flushing the mind of busy thoughts. Peterson calls it a "left brain discourse" (*Take and Read*, p. 8). I'm not sure I could answer my own question as I explore the depth of *The Cloud*, but I work at it and find that simple exercise helps deepen my life. I greatly appreciate how a longtime friend of my family described her own reading habit. She has been a reader of novels for years, but recently has begun exploring some of the great Christian writers. My friend has been tackling C.S. Lewis. Several years ago she acknowledged that Lewis had stretched her and she didn't always understand him. I asked her, "What do you do when you don't understand what he is saying?" She said, "I read until I come to a word, a line, or some sentence that I do understand and I think about that."

The second question is this: *Have I sufficiently scanned the book that I know what it is about?* This is the inspectional level of reading (Adler, p. 18). Adler and Van Doren refer to this as "skimming systematically" (p. 18). In the elementary level the reader is wondering about specific sentences and their meaning. In the inspectional level the reader is asking a larger question: What is the book about? At this level I give the book a good look. I'll scan the title page and preface. What can I find out about the book just by slowing down and meditating on the title? I'll explore the table of contents. If

there is an index I'll stroll through it. I'll even read the dust cover or publisher's blurb. You may be asking, "Can't a reader do both the elementary and inspectional levels of reading simultaneously?" The answer is, "Yes." Good readers are both students and detectives. Adler and Van Doren are helpful: "If your aim in reading is to profit from it—to grow somehow in mind or spirit—you have to keep awake. That means reading as actively as possible. It means making an effort—an effort for which you expect to be repaid" (p. 45). On a practical level, this kind of reading calls me to underline, to write comments and questions in the margin, to highlight, etc. Here, of course, I am assuming that the book is mine and doesn't belong to someone else!

What is this book really about?

The third question is: *What is this book really about?* This kind of reading is called analytical reading and is "preeminently for the sake of understanding" (Adler, p. 19). At this level the reader asks multiple questions. What kind of book is this? What is the underlying skeleton of this work? Is there a problem or problems that the author is trying to solve? What are the key words and significant sentences? What are the book's strengths

C.S. Lewis: "To enjoy a book . . . thoroughly, I find I have to treat it as a sort of a hobby and set about it seriously. I begin by making a map on one of the end leafs: then I put in a genealogical tree or two. Then I put a running headline at the top of each page: finally I index at the end all the passages I have for any reason underlined. I often wonder—considering how people enjoy themselves developing photos or making scrapbooks—why so few people make a hobby of their reading in this way. Many an otherwise dull book which I had to read have I enjoyed in this way, with a fine-nibbed pen in my hand: one is making something all the time and a book so read acquires the charm of a toy without losing that of a book."
The Letters of C.S. Lewis to Arthur Greeves (February 1932), p. 438

C H A P T E R F O U R

Books

and weaknesses? Does this book matter? Why do I agree or disagree with the author? There is a spirit of respectful conversation that hopefully takes place at the analytical level. Sometimes the conversation is so rich and full that it continues on for years between the author and the reader. For some time I have returned to Brother Lawrence and *The Practice of the Presence of God*. I can't tell you how many times I have read it. *The Practice* is one of those devotional classics that could be read in an hour or so, but pondered and considered over the course of one's entire life. It is nothing short of amazing that a seventeenth-century illiterate monk, whose friends jotted down his words and thoughts, could have such a lasting impact on so many, including me!

The final level of reading is what Adler and Van Doren call the syntopical level (p. 20). I have sometimes crafted my own word to describe this kind of reading. I have referred to it as "synthetical" reading. I call it "synthetical" because this level of reading is an attempt to synthesize, to bring together, what has been read and is being read. My word, of course, won't be found in most dictionaries. I have reminded my students on occasion that this is the most difficult and complex form of reading.

"The inventory of philosophical vocabulary used in classical China to define this kind of 'knowing' tends to be one tracing out, unraveling, penetrating, and getting through . . . to trace out the connections among [an idea's] joints and sinews, to discern the pattern in things, and, on becoming fully aware of the changing shapes and conditons of things, to anticipate what will ensue from them." R.T. Ames, Introduction to *The Art of Warfare* by Sun-Tzu, pp. 56-57

The fourth question for the reader is this: *How does this book relate to what I have read elsewhere?*" I have broadened the question at times for my students by asking them to include their own experiences from other media besides

CHAPTER FOUR

Books

the printed page. These experiences might involve what they have heard or what they have seen on television or cinema. This is comparative investigation. The preeminent question, however, that must be asked after everything else has been asked is: Where is God in this book?

For nonreaders, a book is nothing but paper and ink bound together for decoration or dust collection. They cannot imagine the joy and wonder of opening a book and sitting for hours lost in a strange world of words and ideas. The printed word once held a revered place in the American culture. Neal Postman asserts this in *Amusing Ourselves to Death.*

> The farm boy following the plow with book in hand, the mother reading aloud to her family on a Sunday afternoon, the merchant reading announcements of the latest clipper arrivals—these were different kinds of readers from those of today. There would have been little casual reading, for there was not a great deal of time for that. Reading would have had a sacred element in it, or if not that, would have at least occurred as a daily or weekly ritual invested with special meaning (p. 61).

To those of us who have an ongoing love affair with books, that same paper and ink become the door and latch into a world filled with laughter and tears, joy and sorrow, wisdom and stupidity. Consider and weigh these words of Ravi Zacharias.

> I am absolutely convinced that the books one reads possibly help mold one's life more purpose-fully and eternally than we ever realize. . . . May I propose three vital strengths that reading imparts to the life of a person, and the cautions that per-tain. . . . First of all, our Lord Himself reminded us

of the superiority of the word, even to that of the miraculous event. . . . Second, ideas that come through reading give us the privilege of the sovereignty of our own imagination. . . . When we lose the power to read . . . life becomes monotonous and imprisons us in the desolation of our own little sounds. Finally (and this is more a hazard than a gain), reading merely as a conduit for impressing other people is somewhat akin to a sprinkler in a garden that sends forth distant drops of nourishment, but leaves the immediate terrain hard, dry and unproductive ("Bring Me the Books" in *Just Thinking*, p. 2. www.rzim.org).

What kind of reader do you want to be? A good question is worth a thousand answers.

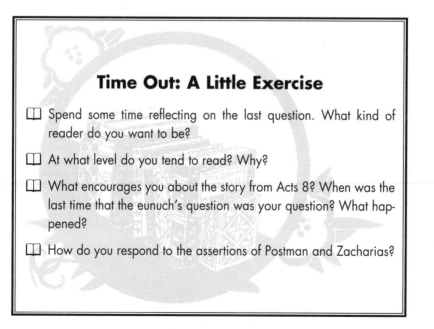

Time Out: A Little Exercise

☐ Spend some time reflecting on the last question. What kind of reader do you want to be?

☐ At what level do you tend to read? Why?

☐ What encourages you about the story from Acts 8? When was the last time that the eunuch's question was your question? What happened?

☐ How do you respond to the assertions of Postman and Zacharias?

5

Reading the Dead Guys

Nothing can exceed the practice of prayer or the devotional reading of Scripture in one's daily devotions. Yet both of these practices need reinforcement and orientation from the example of others, from the sharing of their experiences. Perhaps the devotional use of Scripture is disappearing so fast that it can be rediscovered and made common practice today only with the help of other books. The results of such readings are often far-reaching. In fact, the accidental encounters with great classics of faith and devotion have triggered a whole series of unforeseen reactions
(James Houston, "A Guide to Devotional Reading"
in *The Best in Theology*, vol. 1, p. 271).

My spirit resonates with something David Hansen said in *Leadership* magazine a few years ago. "I mostly read dead people. Reading things that are old delivers me from the feeling of information overload. So much of what's promoted now will be gone in three or four years" (*Leadership*, Spring 1995, p. 125). Students sometimes walk with me from class to class and ask private questions. In one of my classes I had been discussing the need for recovering the great devotional classics. I was pleading with my students to pay attention to those authors whose works have long outlived their own time. These giants are worthy of our hours and attention. I don't know what caused the student to ask this question, but I have delighted in it since. He asked, "Why do you read those dead guys?" What he was really looking for was motivation for his own reading of those deceased writers. There are multiple answers to that student's good question.

In my seminary days one of my professors required the reading of one devotional classic for his class. I chose to explore William Law's, *A Serious Call to a Devout and Holy Life*. This was my first step into the world of the classics. I was hooked from day one. Though Law at times seemed argumentative and legalistic to me, I nevertheless found a connection between the challenges he faced in eighteenth-century England and those I face in twenty-first-century America. I have continued my own pilgrimage into this ancient world of writers for several reasons. Here are some of the explanations for why I continue to read the dead guys.

Why Read the Dead Guys

First, I want to read books that are not bound by time and culture. It is not that I don't read contemporary books; I do read them. I need to hear from my peers and those who are reflecting on postmodern culture. But what I'm particularly interested in is truth. Specifically, I am interested in timeless truth. Susan Muto shares a wonderful illustration. She offers Teresa of Avila's *Interior Castle* as an example of a book that is timeless and unbound by culture (*A Practical Guide to Spiritual Reading*, p. 36). This sixteenth-century mystic was a member of a Spanish family living in Avila. Teresa entered into the life of a Carmelite nun. She heard God's call primarily through her own reading and through struggling with ill health. Her most superb work deals with imagery from medieval times: the castle, the knight, and the lady. As we read the book, we learn that the castle is the heart filled with numerous recesses where God wants to dwell, the knight is God, and the lady is the soul seeking and being sought by God. Though the imagery is time bound, the message is timeless. I am the Bride of Christ who longs for a deeper relationship with the Bridegroom. We all ache for that same intimacy in the inner core of our soul.

Brother Lawrence, the stumbling and fumbling soldier who winds up encountering God in a seventeenth-century monastery kitchen, can speak to me of practicing the presence of God in the twenty-first century. Madame Jeanne Guyon, the suffering spiritual director and writer in seventeenth-century France, can teach me about the way of persistence in the true journey of the Christian life. Thomas à Kempis, the late fourteenth-century and early fifteenth-century German Christian, can instruct me in my desire to imitate Christ. Nee Shu-Tsu, better known as Watchman Nee, the twentieth-century Chinese disciple who was arrested and imprisoned for twenty years, can offer profound help in my desire to live the crucified life. All of these examples and more provide the reader with a vast library of spiritual insight that walks out of specific countries and cultures into our own. This kind of writing has been tried and found to be worth the wait.

C.S. Lewis's caution about modern writing is helpful. A new book so often reflects the fads of our marketplace-driven culture.

> A new book is still on trial, and the amateur is not in a position to judge it. . . . The only safety is to have a standard of plain, central Christianity ("mere Christianity" as Baxter called it), which puts the controversies of the moment in their proper perspective. Such a standard can only be acquired from old books. It is a good rule, after reading a new book, never to allow yourself another new one till you have read an old one in between. If that is too much for you, you should read an old one to every three new ones (*God in the Dock*, pp. 201-202).

There is a second reason why I read the "dead guys." I want to read books that keep me from spiritual flabbiness

and obesity. There is a need for zesty, robust, and athletic spirituality. This is why writers like Blaise Pascal, Ignatius Loyola, John Bunyan, Bernard of Clairvaux, St. Nikodimos and St. Makarios, John Woolman, Dietrich Bonhoeffer, Evelyn Underhill and so many others are essential trainers in our pursuit of spiritual health. Some of what these saints write about we would not agree with, but they have earned the right to be heard because of their contributions. They come from diverse religious backgrounds. They are Catholic, Greek Orthodox, Quaker, and Protestants of various kinds and flavors. If we only read those authors that we agree with, we will never come to that place where our faith is truly grounded. Tozer put it this way:

If we only read those authors that we agree with, we will never come to that place where our faith is truly grounded.

> If I can retain my faith in Christ only by closing my mind against every criticism, I give positive proof that I am not well convinced of the soundness of my position. The person who has had a saving encounter with God is sure beyond the possibility of a doubt. Such a man will not need to shield himself from the classics nor from comparative religions, philosophy, psychology, or science (*The Size of the Soul*, p. 32).

Many of us are looking for books that we can ponder and explore in the years to come. If Jesus tarries, we want something that helps to build muscles of faith that can endure our contemporary challenges. We want something that will have substantial impact upon our worldview and our service to Jesus. What E.M. Bounds has done for my prayer life is nothing short of miraculous. This nineteenth-century

C H A P T E R   F I V E

Books

preacher and Civil War confederate chaplain has spoken to me as clearly as if he were my next door neighbor. His insights and guidance have blessed and built up my inner life. I want to read authors like that.

There is at least one more reason why I read the "dead guys." I want to read books that foster in me a life of trust and obedience. Augustine's life was shipwrecked with sin and disillusionment until he met Jesus. His *Confessions* offer me hope about my own sordid past. John Bunyan was mean-spirited and carried with him the unholy habit of swearing. I need his *Pilgrim's Progress* to give me hope that I can make that long journey toward the Celestial City. Bunyan's classic has been translated into over 198 languages! Apparently people from all walks of life have been helped as much as I have.

Francis Bacon: "Paraphrasing Francis Bacon, one may say that superficial and egocentric knowledge leads to atheism, while genuine, deep, and objective study leads to faith in God."
Eric Charles Barrett,
Scientists Who Believe, p. 9

James Houston, professor of spiritual theology at Regent College, believes that there are no innocent readers ("A Guide to Devotional Reading" in *The Best in Theology*, vol. 1, pp. 273-275). He means that there is no such thing as "just reading." We need the kind of reading that trains us and cheers us on into a life marked by the cross of Christ. Reading is never innocent. It is either drawing us toward Jesus or away from Jesus. We are so bombarded with television, videos, and cinema that we become drowsy in our pursuit of God. We need good books.

Some Practical Suggestions

1. Pray. Ask God to lead you to the right book and author.

C
H
A
P
T
E
R

F
I
V
E

2. Begin. Keep it simple and uncomplicated. Select a classic of such size and interest that you will be motivated to read it through. Talk with someone you know who reads the classics. Ask for some help in getting started. If you don't have a friend like that, begin by reading something brief, for example, Brother Lawrence's *The Practice of the Presence of God*.

3. Don't hurry. This kind of reading is to be savored. Richard Foster once shared that he was reading through *Imitation of Christ*. He was only reading a paragraph a day! Speed is not the point. Deep reflection and transformation are.

4. Remember the four questions I mentioned in chapter four. I sometimes write them into the front of the book I'm reading and record my answers to those questions there. I don't do this as much now as I used to do, because these questions have become so much a part of my life.

> There are no innocent readers; no such thing as "just reading."

5. Dialogue with the author. Keep your pen in hand. Mark the book. Write down your questions in the margins. Pray over what you hear the author saying. Talk to a friend about what you are discovering. Read the book again. If it is worth reading once, it is worth reading twice. Sadly, it never enters the mind of most Christians that a "dead guy" could actually become a spiritual director and mentor for life.

I recall a time when I was pursuing a graduate degree at Friends University in Wichita, Kansas. I would make the long, four-hour drive between Joplin, Missouri, and Wichita

CHAPTER FIVE

each Monday. All of my courses were offered from 6:00 to 10:00 p.m. week after week. It took me two-and-a-half years of nonstop study to complete that degree program. It was the lengthy drive home that tested me. I would get so sleepy and try all kinds of devices to keep myself alert. I drank coffee, sang, ate, rolled down the car window, slapped myself in the face, got out and stretched, and even talked to myself. The best remedy, however, was the one my wife provided. She would periodically recruit a friend to travel with me. That friend made all the difference. I stayed alert and on task because of a traveling companion. That is exactly what the right author and the right book can do for each of us, even if he is a dead guy.

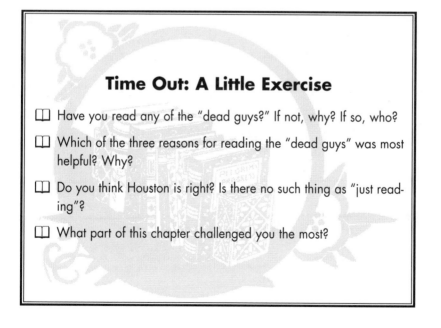

Time Out: A Little Exercise

☐ Have you read any of the "dead guys?" If not, why? If so, who?

☐ Which of the three reasons for reading the "dead guys" was most helpful? Why?

☐ Do you think Houston is right? Is there no such thing as "just reading"?

☐ What part of this chapter challenged you the most?

C
H
A
P
T
E
R

F
I
V
E

6

Surfing the Net, Not the Soul

Meditation is the activity of calling to mind, and thinking over,
and dwelling on, and applying to oneself, the various things that
one knows about the work and ways and purposes and promises of God.
It is an activity of holy thought, consciously performed in the
presence of God, under the eye of God, by the help of God;
as a means of communion with God
(J.I. Packer, *Knowing God*, p. 18).

People who seek the deeper life in this electronic age know the challenge they face. Our society does not tend to applaud the long obedience required to conform to the image of Jesus. We live in a time of instant gratification. If something can't be done quickly, we often find ourselves uninterested. The computer, as wonderful as it is, has helped to foster a spirit of impatience. If we can't get on-line quickly or find that web site immediately, we become frustrated, even angry. Surfing the net can be fun, as long as we use wisdom in where we travel across cyberspace. However, the geography and ocean of the soul cannot be surfed if we are to cultivate depth and substance. This is where reading with God in mind can be of such enormous help.

Tozer has been one of those voices that has blessed and challenged me to produce deeper roots. Though he has been dead since 1963, he continues to shape my thinking and inspire me to read the timeless books slowly. He gives two fundamental reasons why so many present-day Christians shy away from the great classics.

First, present day evangelical Christianity is not producing saints. . . . To come to our devotions straight from carnal or worldly interests is to make it impossible to relish the deep, sweet thoughts found in the great books we are discussing here. . . . Secondly, people are unable to appreciate the great Spiritual classics because they are trying to understand them while having no intention to obey them (*The Size of the Soul*, pp. 48-49).

There is a great deal of debate about the influence of electronics on reading and the reader. Some believe books suffer no ill effects from electronics. Walter Ong would agree, "Despite what is sometimes said, electronic devices are not eliminating printed books but are actually producing more of them" (*Orality and Literacy*, p. 135). Others loudly cheer the negative impact electronics has had on the written word. The very existence of books and their place in contemporary society is being called into question by those who preach the glory and wonder of the electronic age (see Nicholas Negroponte, *Being Digital*). Some, like Sven Birkerts, a highly respected American scholar and author, believe that the decline of "print culture" is producing devastating and tragic results in our time (see *The Gutenberg Elegies*). Barry Sanders, author of *A is for Ox*, sees a link between the collapse of literacy and the rise of violence in the electronic age. He argues that in the end "the computer moves them (students) closer and closer to illiteracy. It breaks the human connections and reinforces the broken connections at home" (p. 128).

The very existence of books and their place in contemporary society is being called into question.

CHAPTER SIX

BOOKS

Most electronic pieces of gadgetry hum with a low level of electricity that continually runs through their circuitry—even when the switch is off. One can hear it pulsing from deep inside most machines. It's alluring, enticing in its promise of life. . . . The world of real presences is fast fading. To recover it means to turn back to books. The electronics industry pours millions of dollars into marketing research and sales strategies. Books cannot stand up against such a force. . . . In some schools, the day begins with students watching the news, and listening to commercials, on Channel One, large-screen television. They start out the day with an electronic feast (Sanders, p. 147).

I'm not sure I agree with Sanders. Perhaps books can and will stand up to the electronic industry. Who knows? Who is correct? Does it even matter? Is there something fundamentally at stake about the soul in the whole discussion?

The Size of the Soul

The size and vitality of the inner life is determined by the transforming work of God the Holy Spirit and our own desire to collaborate with His purposes. A three-year-old girl with braided hair, pierced ears, deep brown eyes, and dressed all in pink, will ask her mom, "Will you read this to me?" The mother looks down at this sweet child and sees a book in her tiny hand. What does that parent do? Perhaps she will take the child into her arms, place that girl on her lap and begin to read. The two of them will revel in each other's company. That's the nature of that kind of relationship. The bond between God and we who seek Him is similar. Those of us who read constantly come to our heavenly

Father and ask Him to speak to us. We long to hear His voice, His heart, His purpose in what we read. In some way that I do not totally comprehend we ask Him, "Will you read this to me?" The problem with the electronic age is that it encourages the discovery of information, not wisdom. Our day encourages skimming, rather than digging. Birkerts, who is not a theologian, nor a writer addressing a Christian audience, puts it this way:

> No deep time, no resonance; no resonance, no wisdom. The only remaining oases are churches (for those who still worship) and the offices of therapists. . . . Fewer and fewer people, it seems, have the leisure or the inclination to undertake it [reading]. And true reading is hard. Unless we are practiced, we do not just crack the covers and slip into an alternate world. We do not get swept up as readily as we might be by the big-screen excitements of film. But if we do read perseveringly we make available to ourselves, in a most portable form, an ulterior existence. We hold in our hands a way to cut against the momentum of the times (*The Gutenberg Elegies*, p. 76).

Our day encourages skimming, rather than digging.

No single writer has challenged my thinking about the essential place of reading books, especially reading them slowly while savoring the words, like Birkerts. I realize my own viewpoint about the place of reading is highly subjective. Many people, not like me, shrug their shoulders at the thought that there is any difference between print communication and electronic media. The point of this book is not to argue about those clear differences. The essence of this humble chapter is to invite the reader to realize that there is

CHAPTER SIX

BOOKS

a fundamental difference between screen and book. "Screen and book may exhibit the same string of words, but the assumptions that underlie their significance are entirely different depending on whether we are staring at book or a circuit-generated text" (Birkerts, p. 128). Language erodes, historical perspectives fade, and the private world begins to vanish as the electronic age accelerates (pp. 128-132). Perhaps I am only a melancholy lover of books, or perhaps the language of the printed page "is the soul's ozone layer and we thin it at our peril" (Birkerts, p. 133).

What I am after is deep reading. I am in pursuit of the meditative and unhurried kind of reading that enlarges my soul for Him. I can't read the great devotional classics at the same rate of speed I read my e-mail or the morning paper. My soul desperately needs a contemplative pace. Birkerts describes the average day of the typical American worker as well as anyone.

> Perhaps the language of the printed page "is the soul's ozone layer and we thin it at our peril"

> He wakens to the sound of the clock radio, pads to the bathroom where he shaves his bristles to the background noise of a television news program, which tells him every minute what time it is and updates him almost as often on the weather. He finishes his coffee while he ties his tie, blasts a croissant in the microwave and carries it along to the car to enjoy on his way to work. The electric garage door lifts, the machine eases forth. Through tinted window glass he notes the look of the sky. The radio has more talk of the weather, some chatter about last night's ball game. He thinks about his office day as he hurtles along the expressway, zeroes in on priorities as he guides the car down the ramp into the office garage. An

CHAPTER SIX

BOOKS

elevator then carries him into the building, and the business day begins. Check e-mail, listen to stored messages. Hours pass as he swivels in front of his computer. The long day unfolds in carpeted and climate-controlled rooms, under the crackle of fluorescents. If he has the energy, he takes an hour for racquetball. A yogurt and a roll. More calls, more moving of data. And as the sun sets over the glass towers of his metropolis, he hurries home to dinner, some Nintendo with the kids, and a few cold ones in front of "NYPD Blue." There are days, quite a few in fact, when our man does not set foot in what used to be known as the outdoors (pp. 205-206).

There is a clear need for physical fitness in this hypothetical man's life, but even more, there is the acute urgency for exercise of the soul (1 Tim 4:7-8). We are being diminished by this electronic age. I believe we are advancing ourselves technologically toward spiritual starvation and smiling all the way, amusing ourselves to death (Postman, p. 4). I know it can sound ludicrous to some for me to suggest that a book of substance, alongside the Scriptures, might help stem the tide of shallowness. But that is exactly what I am claiming. I hunger to read the great ones with God in mind. If I could sustain that holy habit, by grace, maybe I could grow in my love of God. Perhaps my love for God might even blossom into deeper love for my neighbor. This is where I stand.

**C
H
A
P
T
E
R

S
I
X**

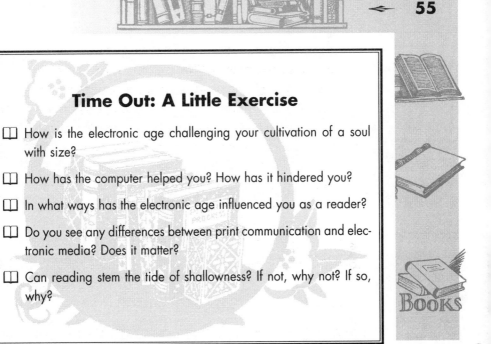

Time Out: A Little Exercise

☐ How is the electronic age challenging your cultivation of a soul with size?

☐ How has the computer helped you? How has it hindered you?

☐ In what ways has the electronic age influenced you as a reader?

☐ Do you see any differences between print communication and electronic media? Does it matter?

☐ Can reading stem the tide of shallowness? If not, why not? If so, why?

7

Reading Your Life

> I was rescued by books. I don't know whether it was because I had impressed them as an employee, or because they couldn't bear to watch me sulking by the remainder stacks. . . . The books that matter to me— and they are books of all descriptions—are those that galvanize something inside me. I read books to read myself (Birkerts, pp. 57 & 102).

My life has been chiseled and polished by the books I have read. I am quite sure that I am not aware of all the myriad of ways God the Spirit has formed and transformed me through my reading. I am sure of this one thing. I read books only to discover that I am reading my own life. I appreciate the encouragement of Charles Spurgeon. He once wrote, "However scant your library, you can study yourself . . . for the most difficult book you will ever read is your own heart" (*Spurgeon's*

I read books only to discover that I am reading my own life.

Lectures to His Students, p. 167). Fred Buechner, one of the superb writers of our own time, invites all of us to carefully read our own journey. Fundamentally reading is listening.

> Listen to your life. See it for the fathomless mystery that it is. In the boredom and pain of it no less than in the excitement and gladness: touch, taste, smell your way to the holy and hidden heart of it because in the last analysis all moments are key moments, and life itself is grace (*Listening to Your Life*, p. 2).

Parker Palmer, writer, teacher, and activist, echoes Buechner's invitation.

> How we are to listen to our lives is a question worth exploring. In our culture, we tend to gather informa-

tion in ways that do not work very well when the source is the human soul: the soul is not responsive to subpoenas or cross-examinations. . . . The soul speaks its truth only under quiet, inviting, and trustworthy conditions. . . . If we want to see a wild animal, the last thing we should do is to go crashing through the woods, shouting for the creature to come out. But if we are willing to walk quietly into the woods and sit silently for an hour or two at the base of a tree, the creature we are waiting for may well emerge, and out of the corner of an eye we will catch a glimpse of the precious wildness we seek (*Let Your Life Speak*, pp. 7-8).

I did not begin my pilgrimage as a reader with much promise. Notes were sent home by my first-grade teacher telling my parents that I was not making satisfactory progress. My mother gently and lovingly coached me to continue trying. I thank God for her. Somewhere, somehow, miraculously I think, the book light came on. I would walk to the tiny public library in the small Midwestern town of Heyworth, Illinois, to peruse the stack of books and listen to novels being read by the librarian. My third-grade teacher, Mrs. Yates, so cheered and challenged me to read that my world became larger and fuller. I moved past Dr. Seuss and Aesop. I met Mark Twain, Robert Louis Stevenson, Daniel DeFoe, James Fenimore Cooper, and Charles Dickens. My appetite for reading grew as I did. I discovered Greek and Roman mythology, especially Homer's, *The Odyssey*. Great American biographies began to enthrall me. A book's theme, symbols, and complex characters sharpened my spiritual eyesight.

Somewhere, somehow, miraculously I think, the book light came on.

Every book I read ultimately led me back to pondering Him. I simply loved Jesus. I wanted to be His faithful son. I was buried in Christian baptism August 13, 1961. My boyhood memories are marked with wondering about God. Even on the athletic field of baseball and football, I pondered books and God. I'm sure my coaches were not always pleased with my obvious musings. Yet, it was more than daydreaming. I was beginning that long, delightful expedition of reading with God in mind.

Something Nearly Died

I cannot pinpoint the time or place, but somewhere in those junior-high and high-school years of the 1960s my odyssey was shipwrecked. I only read what was required, and sometimes I failed even to read that. I went to college in the fall of 1971 and read very little, if at all, over the next year. I worked in a tire store in Marshall, Illinois, and nearly wilted away spiritually. I tried to read Scripture, but it was a dead book to me. The life I was leading only hardened the soil of my heart. Shamefully, I confess I lived the prodigal's life. The dark world of my soul was hidden away. There are always, however, those few people who enter our lives and spy out the landscape of the inner life. These secret agents know what to do, even when we ourselves don't. Mrs. Harper, whom I affectionately refer to as "Mom Harper," was one of those people who probed and prodded my soul. Her husband was my employer and mentor at the tire shop. It is not that Mom Harper directly challenged me to read again or find my fulcrum, rather she prayed for me and created a world of ideas, questions, and encouragement.

Soon I was in the military and began to read again, especially the Bible. I met a group of men who were serious

C H A P T E R S E V E N

about growing as disciples of Jesus. It seemed to me they read anything and everything. I was enticed by their example and began to memorize portions of Scripture and meditate over what God was placing in my heart. I purchased a Bible at a military bookstore in Bonn, Germany, and read it from cover to cover several times. I discovered the world of C.S. Lewis. I found that there was a whole universe of writers that I had never encountered. My childhood hunger for reading and learning was returning.

When my military service was completed, I entered the world of college life again. This time I devoured not only what was required, but I tackled as much of the recommended reading as I could. Bible college ended and seminary began. Books became the tools of my vocation. The link between Christian ministry and spiritual formation deepened. Richard Foster, Eugene Peterson, Dallas Willard, Phil Yancey, A.W. Tozer, and others began to make their way into my heart and mind. I found the classics or perhaps they found me! Time and space do not permit the telling of how books and life have been wedded so inseparably in me. More education followed as did even more service. Now I am looking at the fifty-year mile marker of my life and wondering if I will have enough time to travel even further into the vast country of books and authors yet to be enjoyed. My wife, my best friend, cannot imagine me apart from books. Her mother, Mom Graham, has become my most determined book finder. She is forever on the prowl to locate that classic that I have not yet read.

There was a season in the whirlwind of books, seminary, and ministry where I believed I could not go on. Criticism, over-work, and little rest took its toll. One Sunday night, after evening worship and a

There was a season in the whirlwind of books, seminary, and ministry where I believed I could not go on.

C H A P T E R

S E V E N

Books

difficult meeting, I thought I was coming apart. I wondered if this was what it was like when a person had a "breakdown." I cried and couldn't stop. My wife took me and our family over to the home of dear friends. Even as I write about this experience, my eyes fill with tears. Those precious people reached into their pockets and gave us all the cash they had and then reached into their loving hearts and offered these wise words, "Get out of the area code and let us know where you are." We loaded the car and drove all night spending the next couple of weeks in Arkansas with my wife's parents. I didn't think I wanted to go back to that ministry or to that church. My soul was dry, my mind dull, and my heart broken. My mother-in-law knew better than I did what was happening and what was at stake. For several days I said very little and mostly slept. One morning I heard a knock at the door of the bedroom. I didn't answer. The door creaked open and Mom Graham threw me a Snickers candy bar and a book. The only word from her mouth was, "Enjoy." I did not open either gift for a while, but slowly I began to eat the candy bar and then turned my appetite to the book. Mom had found an old copy of *The Biography of David Livingstone*. I devoured it, reading and rereading words, sentences, and paragraphs. Livingstone's life of courage, endurance, and character spoke deeply to my soul. It was as if God himself spoke loudly and firmly through that book, "If Livingstone can persevere, so can you." After some more days of rest we returned, and our most productive years of ministry in that church followed. One book read with God in mind made all the difference.

Going Inward

John Muir, one of the most celebrated conservationists and nature writers in American history, was a voracious

CHAPTER SEVEN

reader. He grew up in a harsh, conservative Scottish home. He and his siblings were whipped for every act of disobedience, even playful forgetfulness. The one great solace for Muir was his reading. He called it "magnificent golden blocks of time" (*The Wilderness World of John Muir*, p. 52). The only way Muir's father would permit extensive reading was for John to get up early in the morning. Here is Muir's account.

> That night I went to bed wishing with all my heart and soul that somebody or something might call me out of sleep to avail myself of this wonderful indulgence; and next morning to my joyful surprise I awoke before father called me. A boy sleeps soundly after working all day in the snowy woods, but that frosty morning I sprang out of bed as if called by a trumpet blast, rushed downstairs, scarce feeling my chilblains [painful, itchy skin caused by exposure to cold], enormously eager to see how much time I had won; and when I held up my candle to a little clock that stood on a bracket in the kitchen I found that it was only one o'clock. I had gained five hours, almost half a day! "Five hours to myself!" I said, "Five huge, solid hours!" I can hardly think of any other event in my life, any discovery I ever made that gave birth to joy so transportingly glorious as the possession of these five frosty hours (p. 52).

John Muir read deeply and widely. He believed that everything he saw was the direct handiwork of God. He was not a bookworm or a book hoarder. He preferred a day's exposure in the mountains to a wagonload of books. But what he read he read well. By the time he was eleven, he had memorized three fourths of the Old Testament and all of the New

C
H
A
P
T
E
R

S
E
V
E
N

Testament. Muir said, "I could recite the New Testament from the beginning of Matthew to the end of Revelation without a single stop" (p. 17). What challenges me deeply and blesses me most is the purity of Muir's vision, as stated in his own words, "I only went out on a walk and finally concluded to stay out till sundown, for going out, I found, was really going in" (p. 311).

> Books are my wilderness. I go out to explore them slowly, carefully with God in mind, and I am finding that my going out is really my going in.

And thus far, so it has been for me. Books are my wilderness. I go out to explore them slowly, carefully with God in mind, and I am finding that my going out is really my going in.

BOOKS

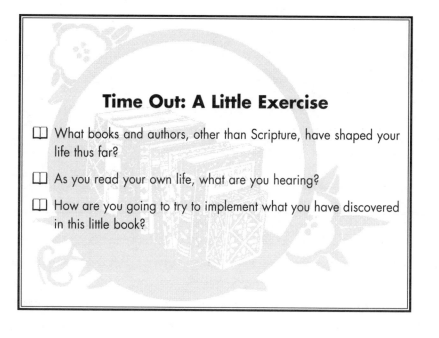

Time Out: A Little Exercise

☐ What books and authors, other than Scripture, have shaped your life thus far?

☐ As you read your own life, what are you hearing?

☐ How are you going to try to implement what you have discovered in this little book?

C
H
A
P
T
E
R

S
E
V
E
N

An Annotated Bibliography

Every reader has their list of favorite books. This one, of course, is my abbreviated version. David McKenna, *How to Read a Christian Book*, and Eugene Peterson, *Take and Read*, offer extensive reading recommendations of their own. I will not seek to duplicate those fine works. Susan Annette Muto's, *A Practical Guide to Spiritual Reading*, remains an excellent resource for the Christian reader as well. Those wanting to find bibliographic help for younger readers from preschool to high school will find Elaine McEwan's book, *How to Raise a Reader*, a gold mine of information. The following books represent for me enduring spiritual classics. This does not mean that other kinds of reading should be avoided. There remains room for reading contemporary authors in every field of study and interest. Novels, newspapers, magazines, and journals should be read in order to know one's culture. The purpose of this book is not to discourage that sort of reading, but to encourage the reading of the devotional classics. The following represents a starting place. Pure Gold Classics Library (Bridge Logos Publishers, Gainesville, FL) has reproduced a number of the classics into contemporary language. Check out their website for reading options: **www.bridgelogos.com**. Here are some of those great books I return to again and again.

Jorge Luis Borges: "I have always imagined that Paradise will be a kind of library."
Jorge Luis Borges, p. 48

Andrews, Lancelot. *Private Devotions*. Gloucester, MA: Peter Smith, 1983.

(16th century) Andrews blesses me in ways that I cannot begin to describe. He grew up in a Puritan home in England and later became a key adviser to King James I. *Private Devotions* was never intended to be published. As the title suggests these are the private prayers from a brilliant man in love with Jesus. This book is a wonderful resource for cultivating a life of prayer of our own.

Anonymous. *The Cloud of Unknowing*. New York: Image Books, 1996 reprint.

(14th century) This unknown writer offers us an insight into the fourteenth-century contemplative movement of England. The book is intended to guide a disciple who has moved past the initial steps all of us make in the life of prayer and now finds that he is in a time of darkness or "unknowing." All of us, at some point in our journey, will come to that same cloudy mist.

Athanasius. *The Life of Antony*. New York: Newman, 1978.

(4th century) I first read Athanasius's reflections on the life of Antony of Egypt when I was a student at Friends University. I was struck by how different these two lives were. Antony entered the monastic life somewhere around AD 271 forsaking everything, Athanasius's (AD 297?-373) journey took him to the city to serve a large congregation in the midst of noise and hurry. I thank God that Athanasius had the wisdom to see the value of telling Antony's story to the world.

Augustine. *The Confessions*. From *The Classics of Western Spirituality*. New York: Image Books, 1960.

(5th century) This book allows the reader to read the journey of one of the foremost thinkers in Church history. They are his autobiographical reflections. Augustine, with humility, traces his own spiritual pilgrimage. I am particularly drawn to his transparent and honest presentation.

BOOKS

B
I
B
L
I
O
G
R
A
P
H
Y

Baillie, John. *A Diary of Private Prayer.* New York: Charles Scribner's Sons, 1949.

(20th century) This Scottish theologian, professor, and author never stopped pursuing a life of devotion. The book is a collection of his private prayers. Thirty-one prayers are offered for morning and night. There are blank pages on the left-hand side across from each written prayer. These pages allow the reader to write their own prayers, record their own reflections, and raise their own questions.

Benedict. *The Rule of St. Benedict.* Collegeville, MN: The Liturgical Press, 1982.

(6th century) *The Rule* is a small but powerful book written by Benedict to give clear, concise, and practical advice to those desiring to live a holy life. He wrote in a time when there were many "religious teachers and gurus" traveling around with little accountability and discipline. One of the most important contributions of the book is the insight it offers about the life of humility.

Bernard. *On the Love of God.* London: A.R. Mowbray, 1961.

(12th century) Bernard, like Augustine, was one of the great leaders in Church history. This book underscores the premiere place of love in the life of the Jesus-follower. Bernard calls us to love God because He first loved us.

Boehme, Jacob. *The Way to Christ.* New York: Harper, 1947.

(17th century) Boehme was a German mystic who wrote about evil as a necessary antithesis to good. *The Way to Christ* helps the reader to see the reality of both.

Bonhoeffer, Dietrich. *Life Together.* San Francisco: Harper, 1954.

(20th century) Of course, anything by Bonhoeffer is worthy of time and attention. This particular book is listed in the bibliography primarily because of the context which gave it birth. Bonhoeffer had gathered around him a number of seminary students at Finkenwald, Germany, during the Nazi's reign of terror. They stud-

ied, prayed, served, and witnessed together in a time of great crisis. The book focuses on one of the central ingredients to spiritual formation: community. *The Cost of Discipleship* should also be included (New York: Macmillan and Collier, 1963).

Bounds, E.M. *Power through Prayer.* Grand Rapids: Baker, 1985 reprint.

(19th century) I return to this book regularly and often because it reminds me of the intimate connection between preaching and prayer.

Brainerd, David. *The Journal of David Brainerd.* Chicago: Moody, 1949 reprint.

(18th century) Here is the story of a courageous, tireless missionary to the American Indian. His life has inspired thousands and had profound impact on Jonathan Edwards, John Wesley, and William Carey.

Brother Lawrence. *The Practice of the Presence of God.* Grand Rapids: Fleming H. Revell, 1993 reprint.

(17th century) Nicolas Herman was born in Lorraine, France, in 1605. Growing up in a very poor family left him without formal education. However in 1666, at the age of 50, he entered the monastery and was given the name Brother Lawrence. This book was first published in 1691 with the simple purpose of recording the thoughts and practices of Brother Lawrence that might be of benefit to others. Fellow monks compiled them after interviewing Lawrence. Over the years many sought Lawrence's advice and wisdom concerning what he meant by giving simple attention to God. This book is a response to that lifelong exercise in spiritual formation. Lawrence's work remains one of my all-time favorites.

Brother Ugolino di Monte Santa Maria. *The Little Flowers of St. Francis.* Garden City, NY: Image, 1958.

(13th century) I sometimes laugh out loud when I read this book—not out of disrespect, but out of a childlike wonder that God could and would use someone as unique and strange as Francis of Assisi. Most historians acknowledge that *Little Flowers* is a combination of legend and fact. The book is filled with glimpses into the world of humility, poverty, prayer, and simplicity. I need regular doses of all four.

Bunyan, John. *The New Pilgrim's Progress: John Bunyan's Classic Revised for Today with Notes by Warren Wiersbe*. Grand Rapids: Discovery House, 1989.

(17th century) No list of devotional classics or resources in Christian spirituality would be complete without this one. This magnificent Christian allegory was written three hundred and twenty-five years ago. However, *Pilgrim's Progress* remains timeless in its simple call to continue journeying until one's walk is finished. Spiritual formation is a lifelong progress.

Cartwright, Thomas. *The Holy Exercise of a True Fast*. London: Unknown Publisher, 1610.

(17th century) I have only read excerpts from this great work. I long to read all of *True Fast*. This is the book on the subject of fasting that has outlasted all the others. In the meantime, I'll continue to look for my copy.

Chambers, Oswald. *The Complete Works of Oswald Chambers*. Grand Rapids: Discovery House, 2000.

(20th century) I read this wonderful and extensive work on a mission trip several years ago to Papua New Guinea, Australia, and New Zealand. What a delight! Chambers was a pastor-teacher whose life was exemplary. He spoke with fire and compassion. Thank God that his wife had the wisdom and the prompting of the Spirit to record and publish his words.

Chesterton, G.K. *Orthodoxy*. London: Fontana Books, 1961.

(20th century) Chesterton, in his own humorous, irony-filled, personal way, presents a set of mental pictures that describes

BIBLIOGRAPHY

what he has come to believe. He calls the book "a sort of sloven-ly autobiography." I love listening to his good mind present his own story.

De Caussade, Jean-Pierre. *The Sacrament of the Present Moment.* San Francisco: Harper and Row, 1982.

(18th century) There are two ideas that surface in De Caussade's book that compel me to read it. First, he invites me to surrender to the will of God, and second, to awaken to God's presence every moment of every day. His example and counsel in these two essential acts of discipleship challenge me to pur-sue God with all of my heart.

De Sales, Francis. *Introduction to the Devout Life.* New York: Image, 1989 reprint.

(16th/17th centuries) This Jesuit priest was a prolific writer. What makes *Introduction to the Devout Life* so important and so valuable is that it combines spiritual depth with practical application. Francis was a master of the metaphor who shows us how to remain passionately devoted to God in the everyday stuff of life.

Doherty, Catherine de Hueck. *Poustinia: Christian Spirituality of the East for Western Man.* Notre Dame, IN: Ave Maria Press, 1975.

(20th century) Catherine is a native Russian who came to North America with a heart to help the poor and hungry. This timeless book shows us how to make a good journey as pilgrims of God from Catherine's unique perspective.

Donne, John. *Devotions upon Emergent Occasions.* Oxford: Oxford University Press, 1987.

(17th century) John Donne wrote this book during a life-threat-ening illness. He was already Dean of St. Paul's and an accom-plished writer. These are his meditations while journeying through a dark night of his own soul.

B
I
B
L
I
O
G
R
A
P
H
Y

Books

Fenelon. *Christian Perfection*. Minneapolis: Bethany House, 1975.

 (17th century) Like so many of the great devotional writers, Fenelon's life was one of paradox. On one hand, he was a prominent member of the French court of Louis XIV. On the other hand, he was a committed disciple who understood that the joyful spiritual life was found in detachment from the things of the world. This book is Fenelon's offering of spiritual direction for those who long for the yoke that is light and the burden that is easy. He was a friend of Madame Guyon.

Fox, George. *The Journal of George Fox*. Cambridge: University Press, 1952.

 (17th century) George Fox was the founder and leader of the Quakers. His journal reveals the life of a bold, compassionate pastor who was not hesitant to call people out of darkness into light.

Grou, Jean-Nicholas. *How to Pray*. Greenwood, SC: Attic Press, 1982.

 (18th century) Grou, like De Sales before him, was a Jesuit priest. The plea of this book is to look to God alone as the One who can and will teach us to pray. I am particularly drawn to his clear and simple advice.

Guyon, Madame Jeanne. *Final Steps in Christian Maturity*. Auburn, ME: Christian Books, 1985.

 (17th century) Madame Jeanne Guyon wrote in a tumultuous time in Catholic France. This book actually represents only a very small part of her vast writings. The Catholic Church destroyed much of her work. Madame Guyon spent nearly two decades in prison because of three massive volumes she authored entitled *The Justification*. This small book is a part of that major endeavor where Guyon attempted to show that she was "justified" for what she had written. Her writings have a very strong mystical leaning. Any reader who is journeying

**B
I
B
L
I
O
G
R
A
P
H
Y**

through a difficult time and wondering how to persist, when God seems so distant, will find this resource an invaluable help. Spiritual formation requires that kind of endurance. *Experiencing the Depths of Jesus Christ* also offers some of the profound insights of Jeanne Guyon.

Hildegard of Bingen. *The Journal of Hildegard of Bingen*. New York: Bell Tower, 1993.

(12th century) Her story is marked by visions from God. She sought the counsel of Bernard of Clairvaux, and he advised her to speak of her visions and prophetic ministry. She lived a full life and wrote extensively until her death at the age of eighty-one. Many readers have found Hildegard's *The Book of Divine Works*, which is a collection of her writings, an invaluable resource for their spiritual quests.

BOOKS

Ignatius. *The Spiritual Exercises of St. Ignatius*. Garden City, NY: Image Books, 1964.

(16th century) Ignatius grew up in a wealthy Spanish family. His early life was marked with strong attachment to the things of this world. As a soldier he received a leg wound in a border dispute with France. His injury required a year of recovery. During that time he read several penetrating books that changed his life, one of which was *The Imitation of Christ. The Spiritual Exercises* is a book that Ignatius wrote during his recuperation. The book represents his instructions on how to take a spiritual retreat. Though there are parts of the book that we might disagree with, his "exercises" have become widely practiced and exceptionally helpful.

John of the Cross. *Ascent of Mount Carmel*. Ligouri, MO: Triumph Books, 1991 reprint.

(16th century) John's *The Dark Night of the Soul* has ministered to millions of readers. The *Ascent* gives us a larger perspective of the long obedience in the same direction that every Christian must

B
I
B
L
I
O
G
R
A
P
H
Y

travel. John was a reformer who was placed in prison because of his views. He wrote about the "dark night" while confined.

Julian of Norwich. *Showings*. (*Revelations of Divine Love*). From *The Classics of Western Spirituality*. New York: Paulist, 1978.

> (14th century) Julian was an English Benedictine nun about whom we know very little. Her book reflects deeply on the goodness of God.

Kelly, Thomas. *A Testament of Devotion*. New York: Harper, 1941.

> (20th century) It was Richard Foster who drew me to Kelly. Richard describes a time when he was waiting for an airplane in a Washington, D.C., airport on a rainy February morning. He was reading Kelly and came upon this line, "We have seen and known some people who seem to have found this deep Center of living, where the fretful calls of life are integrated, where No as well as Yes can be said with confidence." As the rain splattered against the window, Richard's tears splattered against his coat. He realized in that moment that those words were the longing of his own heart (see *Renovare Devotional Readings*, Volume 1, Number 46, p. 4). Those words are the longing of my heart too.

Kempis, Thomas à. *The Imitation of Christ*. New York: Image Books, 1985.

> (15th century) There has been a great deal of debate over the authorship of this great devotional classic. Thomas à Kempis has been popularly recognized as the source. Whether he wrote it or Gerhard Groote did, we are left with a book which seeks to help the reader to live in close communion with God. It uncompromisingly encourages the pursuit of a life of holiness. It does not argue for a life of discipleship, rather it merely assumes that the reader will agree that following Christ is the one, true commitment for the Christian. It has been read for five centuries and continues to remain invaluable as a resource for spiritual formation.

Law, William. *A Serious Call to a Devout and Holy Life*. Philadelphia: Westminster Press, 1978.

(18th century) Law represents one of the finest minds in the early 18th century. This book is vigorous, uncompromising and practical. So many Christians have been greatly influenced and blessed through this devotional classic. The title of the book says it all. Spiritual formation certainly includes an earnest intentionality.

Lewis, Clive Staples. *Mere Christianity*. New York: Macmillan, 1960.

(20th century) Lewis is one of the most important writers and thinkers of the twentieth century. Any of his books are worthy of reading and reflection. This book is one of the finest Christian apologetics ever written.

Luther, Martin. *Three Treatises*. Philadelphia: Fortress Press, 1970 revised edition.

(16th century) It is difficult to select just one of Luther's works. So much of what he wrote continues to impact contemporary Christians. This reformer's mind was brilliant, and his heart remained tender toward God. These three theological treatises represent some of Luther's most famous writings ("Open Letter to the Christian Nobility," "The Babylonian Captivity of the Church," and "The Freedom of the Christian"). The last one is my favorite.

Merton, Thomas. *The Seven Storey Mountain*. New York: Harcourt, Brace and Co., 1948.

(20th century) Very few writers have had such a powerful impact on North American spirituality as Merton. This book is his autobiographical record of his conversion to Catholicism and his ultimate decision to enter a monastic way of life.

Molinos, Michael. *The Spiritual Guide*. Beaumont, TX: Christian Books, 1982.

(16th century) I seldom read Molinos without weeping. This book displays his humble wisdom and spiritual guidance for all true seekers.

His subsequent imprisonment and death continue to preach loudly to those of us who need practical and godly advice for the long haul.

Murray, Andrew. *With Christ in the School of Prayer*. New York: Fleming H. Revell, n.d.

(19th/20th centuries) Murray was a South African missionary preacher of the Dutch Reformed Church. This great book reveals his thoughts on the ministry of intercessory prayer.

Nee, Watchman. *The Normal Christian Life*. Wheaton: Tyndale, 1983 reprint.

(20th century) Nee visited Europe during the years of 1938–39 and gave a series of messages from the book of Romans. Those messages became the basis for *The Normal Christian Life*. In 1952 Nee was arrested and imprisoned in communist China for twenty years. He died June 1, 1972, but his books have remained popular and timeless.

Nouwen, Henri. *In the Name of Jesus*. New York: Crossroad Publishing, 2001.

(20th century) Like many contemporary Christians I find myself coming back to Nouwen again and again. Perhaps it is because he is transparent, vulnerable, concise, and loving. Nouwen was a prolific writer who was passionate about his relationship with God and equally as passionate about the poor, the challenged, and the suffering. He was a Dutch priest who came to North America and taught at some of our most prestigious institutions. The last years of his life were spent ministering to the severely challenged at l'Arche Daybrook community in Toronto, Canada. *In the Name of Jesus* is Nouwen's reflections on Christian leadership based on the temptation of Jesus.

Palmer, Phoebe. *The Way of Holiness*. Salem, OH: Schmul Publishing Co., 1988.

(19th century) In *The Way of Holiness* Phoebe Palmer describes her own experience in seeking to be what she called a "Bible

B
I
B
L
I
O
G
R
A
P
H
Y

Books

Christian." The entire holiness movement of the nineteenth-century cannot be completely understood without some reading and reflection on her writings.

Pascal, Blaise. *Pensees*. New York: Penguin, 1966.
(17th century) I particularly like Os Guinness's edited version (*A Mind on Fire*) of this classic. Pascal was a mathematical genius, an inventor, the great grandfather of the computer and modern risk theory. He also was a man in search of meaning. Not until a fateful near-death experience did he realize that what he longed for was a relationship with God. This book is filled with his thoughts and reflections about the Christian faith. They are random in nature and were not brought together in published form until after his death.

Patrick. *The Confessions of St. Patrick*. New York: Doubleday, 1998.
(5th century). *Confessions* is brief and stirring. Patrick recalls his kidnapping to Ireland, his miraculous escape, and his subsequent calling by God back to Ireland as a missionary. I love this book because of its simple Christ-centeredness.

Rolle, Richard. *The Fire of Love*. New York: Penguin, 1972.
(14th century) Rolle is one of the most energetic and inspiring writers I have read among the great devotional authors. *The Fire of Love* is Rolle's "great symphony" in which he attempts to describe his own love for God with great vividness and repetition.

Smith, Hannah Whitall. *The Christian's Secret of a Happy Life*. Westwood, NJ: Barbour, 1985.
(19th century) Hannah was a Quaker who grew up battling depression and doubt. Through her study of Romans she experienced her victory over these twin giants. In 1875, while living in England, she wrote *The Christian's Secret to a Happy Life*. The book describes the place of surrender and faith in the Christian journey. Her chapter on knowing the will of God is superb.

BIBLIOGRAPHY

Taylor, Jeremy. *The Rule and Exercise of Holy Living.* Boston: Estes & Lauriat, 1875.

(17th century) Few writers have come to understand the importance of sacrifice and humility like Taylor. I am particularly drawn to profound statements like this: "Remember, no one can undervalue you if you know that you are unworthy."

Teresa of Avila. *The Interior Castle.* New York: Paulist, 1979.

(16th century) Teresa delights in metaphor. For her the medieval castle is the perfect analogy for our relationship with God. She invites us to move deeper and deeper into the castle of the soul where we can experience intimacy with God.

Therese of Lisieux. *The Story of a Soul.* New York: Image, 2001 reprint.

(16th century) Therese only lived to be twenty-four years old. *The Story of a Soul* is her autobiography. Millions of copies of this simple and unpolished account have been sold. Just before she died Therese spoke these prophetic words, "What I have written will do a lot of good. It will make the kindness of God better known."

Tozer, A.W. *The Pursuit of God.* Camp Hill, PA: Christian Publications, 1982 reprint.

(20th century) Tozer remains one of my all-time favorite authors. His humble beginnings and his growth as a man in pursuit of God challenge me regularly. Several dozen of his books remain in print. This one continues to be widely read. *The Pursuit of God* reveals the place of the great devotional writers in Tozer's own life.

Trueblood, Elton. *The Company of the Committed.* New York: Harper & Row, 1962.

(20th century) Trueblood assesses culture and the Church like very few can. His books reveal that rare quality of insight that only comes from time spent alone with God. This particular book elevates the essential place of community and witness.

B
I
B
L
I
O
G
R
A
P
H
Y

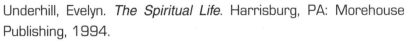

Underhill, Evelyn. *The Spiritual Life*. Harrisburg, PA: Morehouse Publishing, 1994.

(20th century) Underhill never traveled far. Her keen insight comes from study, reflection, and taking care of her garden. This very brief book demonstrates her unusual awareness of the nature of the life of devotion.

Wallis, Arthur. *God's Chosen Fast*. Fort Washington, PA: Christian Literature Crusade, 1968.

(20th century) This twentieth-century writer, relatively unknown, explains the Christian life of fasting with profound clarity.

Wesley, John. *The Journal of John Wesley*. Chicago: Moody, 1951.

(18th century) Here is a giant! This book is a synthesis of the multitude of Wesley's journals. It is worth the read.

Woolman, John. *The Journal of John Woolman and A Plea for the Poor*. Philadelphia: Citadel Press, 1961.

(18th century) Woolman was a humble Quaker who observed and then prayed over the inhuman treatment of slaves in the United States. His *Journal* was written over a period of sixteen years. This quiet, peaceful man describes his travels up and down the East coast imploring other Quakers to free their slaves and embrace the love of God for all people. Few books have touched me as deeply as this one.

B
I
B
L
I
O
G
R
A
P
H
Y

Works Cited

Adler, Mortimer J., and Charles Van Doren. *How to Read a Book.* New York: Simon and Schuster, 1972.

Baillie, John. *A Diary of Private Prayer.* New York: Simon and Schuster, 1996 reprint.

Birkerts, Sven. *The Gutenberg Elegies.* New York: Ballantine Books, 1994.

Bounds, E.M. *Power through Prayer.* Grand Rapids: Zondervan, 1962.

Bradbury, Ray. *Fahrenheit 451.* New York: Ballatine Books, 1982 reprint.

Buechner, Frederick. *Listening to Your Life.* San Francisco: Harper, 1992.

Hanson, David. "The Dead Writers Society." *Leadership.* Carol Stream, IL: Christianity Today, Spring 1995.

Houston, James. "A Guide to Devotional Reading." *The Best in Theology.* Vol. 1. J.I. Packer and Paul Fromer, eds. Carol Stream, IL: Christianity Today, 1999.

Jacobs, Alan. *A Theology of Reading.* Boulder, CO: Westview Press, 2001.

Kempis, Thomas à. *The Imitation of Christ.* New York: Image Books, 1985.

Lewis, C.S. *God in the Dock.* Walter Hooper, ed. Grand Rapids: Eerdmans, 1970.

McEwan, Elaine. *How to Raise a Reader.* Grand Rapids, Baker, 1999 reprint.

McKenna, David L. *How to Read a Christian Book.* Grand Rapids: Baker, 2001.

BOOKS

Means, James. *Effective Pastors for a New Century.* Grand Rapids: Baker, 1993.

Morley, Chris. *Handbook of Contemporary Preaching.* Michael Duduit, ed. Nashville: Broadman Press, 1992.

Muir, John. *The Wilderness World of John Muir.* Edwin W. Teale, ed. New York: Mariner Books, 2001.

Muto, Susan Annette. *A Practical Guide to Spiritual Reading.* Denville, NJ: Dimension Books, 1976.

Ong, Walter J. *Orality and Literacy.* New York: Routledge, 1995 reprint.

Packer, J.I. *Knowing God.* Downers Grove, IL: InterVarsity, 1973.

Palmer, Parker. *Let Your Life Speak.* San Francisco: Jossey-Bass, 2000.

Peterson, Eugene. *Take and Read.* Grand Rapids: Eerdmans, 1996.

Postman, Neal. *Amusing Ourselves to Death.* New York: Penguin, 1986.

Sanders, Barry. *A is for Ox.* New York: Vintage Books, 1994.

Spurgeon, Charles. *Spurgeon's Lectures to His Students.* David O. Fuller, ed. Grand Rapids: Zondervan, 1945.

Stott, John. *Guard the Gospel.* Downers Grove, IL: InterVarsity, 1973.

Tozer, A.W. *The Size of the Soul.* Camp Hill, PA: Christian Publications, 1992.

Zacharias, Ravi. "Bring Me the Books." *Just Thinking.* www.rzim.org.

**W
O
R
K
S**

**C
I
T
E
D**